Don't Accept All Thought That Comes to your Mind

Breaking Free From Confirmation Bias

Steven C. Hood

Description

"Don't Accept Every Thought That Comes to Your Mind" is a thought-provoking investigation of the complexities of human cognition and belief systems. The book explores critical thinking, cognitive biases, and self-awareness, challenging readers to question their own beliefs and views. It leads people on a path of comprehending the complexities of their thoughts, encouraging thoughtful introspection and cultivating a more resilient

and open-minded attitude to navigating the world. This book is an excellent resource for anyone seeking personal development, improved decision-making, and a better understanding of the elements that influence their ideas.

Table of contents:

Introduction: 3
CHAPTER 1 3
The Journey to finding the root cause of suffering...............3
CHAPTER 2: 3
The root of suffering..3
CHAPTER 3: 3
Why do we even think 3
CHAPTER 4: 3
Thought vs. Thinking 3
CHAPTER 5: 3
If we can only feel what we're thinking, Don't we need to think positively to feel that way? 3
CHAPTER 6: 3
How the human experience is created - the three principles 3
CHAPTER 7: 3
If thinking is the root cause of suffering, How do we stop thinking? 3
CHAPTER 8: 3
How can we possibly thrive in the world without thinking? 3
CHAPTER 9: 3
If we stop thinking, What do we do about our goals, dreams & ambitions?...3
CHAPTER 10: 3
Unconditional Love & Creation 3
CHAPTER 11: 3
What do you do next after experiencing peace,Joy, Love & Fulfillment in the present ? 3
CHAPTER 12: 3
Nothing is either good or bad 3

CHAPTER 13: 3
How do you know what to do without thinking? 3
CHAPTER 14: 3
How to follow your intuition 3
CHAPTER 15: 3
Creating space for miracles 3
CHAPTER 16: 3
What happens when you begin living in non-thinking (potential
obstacles) ? 3
Conclusion: 3
Description...1

Introduction:

Welcome to this transforming trip through the pages of this book. As you embark on this journey, you will gain important insights about the power of your ideas and how they influence your perceptions, decisions, and general well-being. This book is a roadmap for testing the idea that everything you believe is the ultimate truth. It helps you to examine, ponder, and adopt a thoughtful approach to your cognitive processes.

Throughout these chapters, you will learn about cognitive biases, the impact of views, and the value of self-awareness. By delving into the content, you will get tools for navigating your mind's intricacies and learning how to overcome limiting beliefs.

To get the most out of this experience, go into each chapter with a willingness to learn. Accept the tasks and thoughts as opportunities for personal development. Allow the content to question your assumptions and create a more conscious style of thinking. Whether you're looking for clarity, personal development, or a new viewpoint, this book will help you on your journey to increased self-awareness. As you work through the material, remember that grasping the complexities of your thoughts is an ongoing effort. Take the time to think about your own experiences and be gentle with yourself. The true worth of this exploration is in the insights you get and the good adjustments you may implement in your life. May this path lead to self-discovery, empowerment, and the awareness that you have the capacity to change your beliefs and, as a result, your life. Enjoy the voyage ahead!

CHAPTER 1

The Journey to finding the root cause of suffering

The road to determining the source of sorrow is a profound examination of our inner landscapes. It starts with profound introspection, peeling back the layers of our experiences to find the root causes of our misery. This journey frequently entails confronting our anxieties, admitting suppressed emotions, and challenging old ideas. Along the journey, we may feel uncomfortable and vulnerable, but these are necessary stages toward comprehending the underlying source of our

pain. It necessitates a dedication to self-discovery and a readiness to challenge the narratives we have created about ourselves and the world.
As we go deeper, mindfulness becomes a guiding light, providing a prism through which we can examine our thoughts and feelings without judgment. This increased awareness enables us to recognize patterns and repeated themes, bringing us closer to the source of our discontent.
The road is not linear; it is a continuous process of unwinding, learning, and evolving. It could entail seeking help from others, whether through meaningful talks, therapy, or spiritual advice. Connecting with our innermost selves and accepting the possibility of transformation requires courage.

Finally, identifying the source of pain is a transforming journey that enables us to make conscious choices, develop resilience, and cultivate a deeper feeling of inner peace. It is a continual journey that invites us to be compassionate toward ourselves and others, acknowledging that knowledge and healing are essential components of the human experience.

CHAPTER 2:
The root of suffering

Suffering stems from the intricate web of our desires, relationships, and the ever-changing flow of existence. Suffering is often the result of our aversion to change, which is a natural aspect of the human experience. We seek permanency in an ephemeral environment, clinging to possessions, relationships, and identities. Our insatiable desire for pleasure and avoidance of pain lead to the cycle of suffering. The attachment to pleasure develops a yearning, which, when not met, leads to discontent. In contrast, aversion to pain causes worry and anxiety, maintaining our sense of unease.

Furthermore, our thoughts contribute significantly to misery by engaging in patterns of negative thinking, self-doubt, and incessant comparison with others. The stories we tell ourselves about who we are and who we should be can cause a great deal of stress. According to Buddhist philosophy, the three root causes of suffering are desire, ignorance, and aversion. Craving refers to our wishes, ignorance is a lack of comprehension of reality, and aversion is our opposition to what is. To break free from these roots, one must do a thorough self-exploration, cultivate mindfulness, and accept the impermanence of all things. Recognizing the source of suffering is not about avoiding life's obstacles, but about knowing how we respond to them. We can remove the grip of suffering on our lives by increasing our self-awareness, compassion, and acceptance, allowing us to live more liberated and satisfied lives.

According to numerous philosophical and psychological perspectives, suffering stems from fundamental human experiences such as attachment, aversion, and ignorance.

Attachment is the emotional relationship we make with people, belongings, or circumstances in order to find security and fulfillment

outside of ourselves. The
trouble emerges when
these attachments become
so strong that we fight life's
inevitable changes and
uncertainty. The more we
cling to things, the more we
grieve when they eventually
change or disappear.
Aversion, on the other hand,
is our natural reflex to avoid
pain, discomfort, or
situations that we dislike.
The persistent endeavor to
avoid unpleasant events
can result in tension, worry,
and an endless circle of
dissatisfaction. The refusal
to embrace the ebb and
flow of life contributes
considerably to our sorrow.
Ignorance is a lack of
insight or awareness of the
true nature of reality. This
ignorance can present itself
in a variety of ways,
including failing to recognize
the impermanence of all
things, the interdependence
of life, and the fleeting
nature of pleasure and grief.

When we work under
incorrect assumptions or
misconceptions, we provide
fertile ground for misery to
grow.
Breaking free from the
causes of suffering entails
cultivating mindfulness, or
having a deep awareness of
our thoughts and emotions.
It is about seeing
attachments without getting
chained to them,
confronting aversions
calmly, and removing the
ignorance that distorts our
vision of reality. Meditation,
self-reflection, and a
dedication to continual
learning are all important
steps in this transforming
path toward understanding
and reducing suffering.

CHAPTER 3:

Why do we even think

Thinking is an essential component of human cognition that performs a variety of functions, demonstrating the complexity and adaptability of the human mind. Here are some important reasons why we participate in thinking:

Problem solving: Thinking enables us to examine situations, recognize issues, and devise solutions to overcome hurdles. It's a valuable tool for navigating life's intricacies and solving challenges.

Decision Making: We consider choices, analyze the advantages and drawbacks, and make informed decisions. This

cognitive process assists us in navigating a wide range of options, from minor daily decisions to major life decisions.
Adaptation to the Environment: Thinking is an evolutionary benefit that allows us to adapt to our surroundings.
It entails learning from our experiences, forecasting events, and adapting our behavior in response to feedback and information.
Creativity and Innovation: Thinking stimulates creativity by allowing us to produce new ideas, link dissimilar thoughts, and imagine fresh solutions. It lies at the center of artistic expression, scientific discovery, and technological innovation.
Thinking is inextricably related to language and communication. We use thought to organize ideas, construct messages, and communicate information to

others, promoting social engagement and collaboration.

Reflection and Self-Awareness:
Thinking enables us to consider our experiences, feelings, and behaviors. It promotes self-awareness, allowing us to better comprehend our motives, values, and personal development.

Imagination:
Our ability to think permits us to conceive scenarios beyond the present world. This imaginative thinking serves as the foundation for creativity, narrative, and the pursuit of goals.

Thinking is necessary for the processes of learning and remembering. It entails encoding, storing, and retrieving data, which contributes to our ongoing growth and adaptation.

Problem Anticipation:
Thinking allows us to predict prospective obstacles and

plan for future events. This
proactive way of thinking
enables us to design and
implement preventive
measures.
Existential Contemplation:
Humans contemplate life,
purpose, and meaning.
Contemplative thought is a
distinct component of
human awareness that
motivates philosophical and
spiritual inquiry.
In essence, thinking is a
comprehensive cognitive
tool that allows us to
negotiate the intricacies of
our lives, learn from our
experiences, and
continuously adapt and
innovate in an ever-
changing world.

CHAPTER 4:
Thought vs. Thinking

"Thought" and "thinking" are
interconnected components

of cognition, although they have different features.

Definition of Thought:
Thoughts are mental products such as ideas, opinions, and images. It includes the contents of the mind—what we consciously or unconsciously hold in our awareness.

Nature:
Thoughts can be brief or persistent, logical or emotive. They can be automatic, arising without conscious effort, or purposeful, emerging as a result of focused contemplation.

Thoughts can come from a variety of sources, such as external stimuli, previous experiences, or internal mental processes. They frequently impact our views and influence our emotions and behaviors.

Thinking is the active use of mental faculties to study, analyze, and manipulate information. It entails the use of cognitive functions to investigate ideas, solve problems, and make judgments.

Dynamic Process:

Thinking is a dynamic and intentional action. It demands mental effort and incorporates several cognitive processes, including reasoning, memory retrieval, and problem solving.

Thinking, as opposed to involuntary thoughts, is a more conscious and intentional involvement with mental information. It frequently entails a deliberate focus on a single topic or purpose.

The relationship between thoughts and thinking involves reciprocal influence. Thoughts can trigger the thinking process, leading to careful reflection. In contrast, thinking may change and refine our ideas through logical analysis and reflection.

Continuous Interaction:
Thoughts and thinking
interact constantly in our
regular mental activity.
concepts serve as the basic
material for thinking, and
thinking itself generates
new concepts.
Cognitive Flexibility:
Thoughts can be
spontaneous and automatic,
but they also allow for more
careful and flexible
investigation of concepts. It
offers a systematic
approach to
comprehending, assessing,
and changing mental
content.
In conclusion, thought
reflects the content of the
mind, encompassing
numerous mental
constructs, whereas
thinking is the active and
intentional activity by which
we engage with and alter
that mental material.
In summary, thought
represents the content of
the mind, which includes a

variety of mental constructs, whereas thinking is the active and purposeful activity by which we interact with and manipulate mental content. Both play critical roles in forming our perception of the world and our reactions to it, emphasizing the dynamic and nuanced character of human cognition.

CHAPTER 5:

If we can only feel what we're thinking, Don't we need to think positively to feel that way?

The concept that we can only feel what we believe implies a close relationship between our thoughts and emotions. Indeed, our ideas have a big impact on our emotional states. The premise that positive thinking can lead to positive feelings is based on cognitive and positive psychology principles. Here's an analysis of this relationship:

1. The cognitive-behavioral connection: Cognitive distortions: Cognitive-behavioral therapy (CBT) stresses that our thoughts can be misinterpreted and lead to bad feelings. Recognizing and confronting these distortions can result in more balanced and positive thinking.

2. Pleasant Psychology emphasizes strengths, pleasant emotions, and optimistic thinking. This method seeks to improve well-being and resilience by intentionally focusing thoughts toward good parts of life.

3. **The Power of Mindset:** Fixed vs. Growth Mindset: According to psychologist

Carol Dweck's research, having a growth mindset leads to more positive feelings than a fixed mindset. This demonstrates how our beliefs about our skills influence our emotional experiences.

4. **Emotional Regulation:** Thoughts influence emotions. Emotional regulation is the process of understanding and managing emotions. Recognizing and confronting negative beliefs can be an important part of managing emotions, resulting in a more positive and adaptive emotional experience.

5. **The Effect on Behavior:** Positive thinking can boost motivation and action. When we think favorably about our skills or the result of a situation, we are more likely to take good actions, which contributes to a positive feedback loop of

ideas, emotions, and behaviors.

6. **Realism and Positivity.**
Balancing Realism:
While optimistic thinking can be useful, it is critical to maintain a balance with realistic thinking. Recognizing problems and disappointments realistically while having a cheerful outlook enables a more flexible and nuanced approach to life.

In summary, the link between thinking positively and feeling positive emphasizes the dynamic interplay between thoughts and emotions. However, it's crucial to understand that cultivating a happy mindset does not imply ignoring or repressing bad emotions. Instead, it entails comprehending and managing our ideas in a way that fosters emotional well-being and resilience.

CHAPTER 6:
How the human experience is created - the three principles

The construction of the human experience is frequently viewed through the perspective of the Three Principles, a paradigm that emphasizes the importance of thought, consciousness, and mind in constructing our reality.

 These concepts offer insights into the nature of human experience.

The first premise focuses on the dynamic nature of mind. Thoughts do not remain static; they move through our thoughts, affecting our views and interpretations of the environment.

Influence on Feelings: Our emotions are directly influenced by our thoughts. The nature and substance of our thoughts determine whether we experience positive or negative sentiments. Understanding the fleeting nature of thought can result in a more adaptable and resilient emotional state. Consciousness is the awareness of one's ideas. It enables us to see and comprehend the ongoing flow of mental activity. By being aware of our thoughts, we get the capacity to choose which ones to engage with and which to dismiss.

The third principle, known as Mind, represents the creative power that drives life. It is the origin of all thoughts and consciousness. Understanding our connection to the cosmic mind develops a sense of unity and purpose in the human experience.

Key concepts:

The Three Principles argue that humans have an underlying sense of well-being.

Individuals can tap into their natural well-being, regardless of external circumstances, by comprehending the transient nature of cognition and the role of consciousness.

Resilience and Clarity: When people understand the ideas, they frequently feel more resilient and clear. Recognizing that their thinking shapes the quality of their experience permits them to address life's difficulties with greater openness and responsiveness.

Applications in Daily Life: Mindfulness and presence: Mindfulness correlates with the ideals by encouraging people to be present and cognizant of their thoughts. This awareness allows for a more conscious response to situations.

Understanding the concepts promotes emotional management. When people comprehend that their feelings are reflections of their thinking, they may better navigate and regulate their emotional experiences. In conclusion, the Three Principles provide insight into how the human experience is formed through the interaction of cognition, consciousness, and the universal wisdom of Mind. Recognizing these principles can result in a significant shift in how people see and interact with their ideas, promoting improved well-being and a deeper sense of connection to the larger fabric of life.

CHAPTER 7:
If thinking is the root cause of

suffering, How do we stop thinking?

The notion that thinking is the primary cause of suffering is consistent with many philosophical and mindfulness traditions, implying that excessive or erroneous thinking can lead to emotional pain. While it is not possible to cease thinking entirely—thinking is a natural and necessary element of human cognition—there are ways to create a more conscious and balanced relationship with our ideas. Mindfulness Meditation involves observing without attachment. Mindfulness meditation facilitates noticing thoughts without becoming caught in them. Individuals can acquire a nonjudgmental awareness of their ideas by focusing their attention on the present moment, allowing them to come and go without attachment.

Focused Attention Techniques:

Concentration practices like focused breathing or mantra meditation can reduce scattered thoughts by directing attention to a single point. This focused concentration generates a mental space that promotes clarity and calmness. Mindful awareness in daily life involves bringing presence to activities. Extending mindfulness to regular activities necessitates complete concentration in the present moment. Whether eating, walking, or performing any other normal task, being totally present helps shift the focus away from unnecessary thinking and toward direct sensation.

Cognitive Behavioral Approaches:

Identify and challenge distorted thoughts.

Cognitive-behavioral techniques are used in therapy to help people detect and challenge distorted or negative thinking. Reframing thought patterns allows people to lessen the impact of automatic, inappropriate thinking on their emotions.

Acceptance and Commitment Therapy (ACT): This promotes attentive acceptance of ideas and emotions instead of suppressing or controlling them. This strategy assists individuals in developing a more flexible connection with their thoughts, resulting in increased emotional well-being.

Mind-Body Practices: Yoga, Tai Chi, or Qigong integrate physical movement and breath awareness to foster a mind-body connection. Engaging in these activities can assist to relax the mind and reduce unnecessary thinking.

Journaling and self-reflection provide an organized way to express thoughts and reflect on them. This technique can help people achieve clarity, recognize patterns, and develop a better relationship with their thoughts.

It's vital to highlight that the goal isn't to stop thinking altogether, but rather to build a more thoughtful and discerning approach to thoughts. The activities stated above are intended to create space between the individual and their ideas, resulting in a heightened sense of presence, clarity, and emotional resilience. The idea is to build a conscious and intentional relationship with one's thought processes rather than attempting to fully halt them.

CHAPTER 8: How can we possibly thrive in the world without thinking?

Surviving in the world without thinking is difficult since thought processes influence decision-making, problem-solving, and learning. Critical thinking promotes adaptation and resilience, which are crucial for negotiating life's challenges. Without careful consideration, it may be difficult to appreciate implications, make educated decisions, or comprehend different points of view.

Embracing cognitive engagement improves our ability to thrive in a constantly changing world. Thriving in the world without thinking includes a lack of cognitive engagement, critical analysis, and intentional decision-making. This scenario presents considerable obstacles in several areas of life.

1. Decision-Making: - Lack of thought leads to impulsive and rash decisions.
- Long-term repercussions may be disregarded, leading to adverse results.
- Strategic planning, a result of careful consideration, is jeopardized.

2. Effective problem: - solving requires critical thinking skills to appraise situations, identify challenges, and produce solutions.
- The absence of critical thinking impairs the ability to negotiate complexities and overcome hurdles.

3. Learning and Adaptability:- Thinking helps absorb and integrate new ideas.
- Adaptive behavior is based on the ability to

reflect, analyze, and alter strategies, all of which are cognitive activities.

4. Interpersonal Relationships: - Cultivating empathy and understanding by considering others' views is essential for maintaining successful relationships.

- Without thinking, communication can become insensitive, resulting in misunderstandings and confrontations.

5. Innovation and Creativity:
- Creative thinking, concept exploration, and challenge to the status quo are common drivers of innovation.

- A lack of thinking reduces the potential for new discoveries and innovative solutions.

6. Emotional Regulation: - Thinking helps individuals absorb and respond to emotions constructively. - Without this cognitive component, emotional responses may be

impulsive and uncontrollable.
7. Reflective thinking promotes personal growth through self-awareness and ongoing improvement.
- Thriving in the lack of thought may limit one's capacity for growth and self-realization.
Essentially, flourishing without thinking is like navigating a difficult maze while blindfolded. While fast action may occur, the absence of critical analysis reduces the possibility of favorable consequences. Individuals must embrace cognitive engagement and critical thinking in order to not only survive, but prosper, in today's dynamic and diverse environment.

CHAPTER 9:
If we stop thinking, What do we do about our goals,

dreams & ambitions?

If we stop thinking, our objectives, hopes, and ambitions lose their strategic basis and become elusive aspirations. Thought processes are essential in the pursuit of these goals, impacting our behaviors, decisions, and tenacity.
1. **Clarity of Goals**: Thinking helps clarify and develop our goals.
- Without careful analysis, goals may lack precision and direction, making achievement more difficult.
2. **Planning and Strategy:** - Strategic thinking is essential for creating effective plans and strategies to attain goals.
- A lack of cognitive engagement might lead to a lack of systematic techniques, which impedes advancement.
3. **Motivation and Persistence:** - Thinking

promotes motivation by visualizing desirable outcomes and recognizing the importance of goals.
- Without a cognitive connection to our goals, staying motivated becomes difficult, potentially leading to abandoned pursuits.
4. **Adaptability:** - Thought processes provide flexible responses to changing circumstances. - Individuals who do not actively evaluate issues or new knowledge may find it difficult to modify their tactics.
5. **Decision-Making in Pursuit of Dreams:** - Achieving dreams often requires making crucial choices along the road.
- Thoughtful consideration ensures that actions are consistent with the broader vision, avoiding rash decisions that could derail progress.
6. **Problem-Solving for Ambitious Pursuits:** -

Obstacles in ambitious efforts often require imaginative problem-solving. Without the ability to think through issues, it may be difficult to overcome obstacles and continue moving forward.

7. **Continuous Improvement:** Thoughtful reflection promotes personal and professional progress.

- Stopping to contemplate may impede the learning and progress required for the pursuit of lofty goals.

In essence, every aspect of goal setting and achievement is inextricably linked to cognitive engagement. The absence of thoughtful evaluation jeopardizes the entire process, potentially resulting in unmet objectives and goals. Adopting a proactive and strategic thinking style is critical for translating aspirations into actionable strategies and overcoming the inevitable obstacles on the route to success.

CHAPTER 10:
Unconditional Love & Creation

Unconditional love and creation are tremendous forces that shape the human experience, encouraging deep relationships and promoting personal and social growth.
1. **Unconditional Love:** - Unconditional love accepts individuals as they are, warts and all.
- It requires understanding, compassion, and the willingness to help others without expecting anything in return.
- This type of love fosters a nurturing environment, promoting emotional well-being and strengthening interpersonal ties.

2. **Creation:** - Various forms of creation demonstrate human intellect, invention, and imagination. It includes artistic activities, scientific discoveries, and the formation of relationships and communities.
- The act of creativity is an essential part of human nature, propelling progress and adding new dimensions to our lives.
3. **The Relationship between Unconditional Love and Creation:** - Unconditional love fosters creativity by providing a nurturing foundation for individuals to pursue their creative potential.
- Unconditional love, whether in art, science, or personal relationships, provides a sense of security and freedom to express oneself authentically. In contrast, the act of creation frequently enhances connections and love by

strengthening individual
bonds via shared
experiences and joint
endeavors.
4. **Unconditional love in
partnerships fosters
creativity in problem:** -
solving and managing
problems jointly.
- Couples, families, and
communities thrive when
they adopt innovative
approaches to
communication,
understanding, and conflict
resolution.
5. **Empathy and
Understanding:** -
Unconditional love is linked
to empathy, which helps
people comprehend and
relate to the experiences of
others.
- Empathy, in turn, drives
innovative solutions to
societal problems, fostering
inclusivity and compassion.
6. **Parental Love and
Creativity:** - Parental love
promotes unconditional love
and fosters caring

circumstances for children to grow.

- Children who feel secure in this affection are more likely to be creative in their thoughts, activities, and hobbies.

7. **Global Impact:**- Unconditional love and creation have a greater impact on society than just intimate connections.

- Acts of love and creation, large and small, lead to constructive societal change, innovation, and the betterment of human life. Finally, the interaction of unconditional love and creation creates a harmonious dance that nourishes both individuals and communities. These energies, whether manifested via personal ties, artistic pursuits, or societal progress, are inextricably linked, forming a world in which love drives creativity and creation nurtures love.

CHAPTER 11:
What do you do next after experiencing peace,Joy, Love & Fulfillment in the present ?

After experiencing peace, pleasure, love, and fulfillment in the moment, the next stages are to cultivate and extend these good states while encouraging personal growth and constructively contributing to the world.

1. Gratitude and Reflection:

- Express your thankfulness for the present moments of serenity, pleasure, love, and fulfillment.

- Consider the variables that contributed to these great experiences and what causes a sense of contentment.

2. Mindfulness and Presence: - Practice mindfulness to stay present and appreciate current moments of calm and joy.
- Being aware of the current moment helps to maintain happy feelings and strengthens connections with one's surroundings.
3. Share and Connect: - Share pleasant experiences with loved ones to create a sense of connection and promote optimism.
- Have meaningful interactions in which you can share and receive the joy and fulfillment you've felt.
4. Set and Pursue New Goals: - Utilize the good energy garnered from these experiences to establish new goals and ambitions.
- Use the sensation of fulfillment to fuel personal and professional activities, resulting in a never-ending cycle of growth and achievement.

5. Contribute to Others: - Show love and fulfillment to others by acts of compassion and charity.
- Volunteering or assisting those in need can provide a greater sense of purpose and happiness.
6. Creative Expression: - Use painting, writing, music, or other creative avenues to express happy emotions. Creativity may be a rewarding method to record and express the essence of both happy and tranquil moments.
- Identify areas for further improvement and establish goals for ongoing development.
8. Maintain a Balanced Lifestyle: - Prioritize work, leisure, and self-care for overall well-being.
- Prioritize activities that promote pleasant emotions and avoid pressures that may undermine these experiences.

9. Embrace Change and Adaptability: - Be open to life's natural ebb and flow, accepting challenges as part of the journey.
- Develop resilience and adaptability to face changes with a good attitude.
10. Continued Learning: - Participate in activities that encourage lifelong learning and personal enrichment. - Whether via school, travel, or the pursuit of new hobbies, continuous learning contributes to a sense of fulfillment.
In a nutshell the journey after experiencing peace, joy, love, and fulfillment entails making a deliberate effort to maintain these pleasant experiences while contributing to personal and community well-being. Individuals can continue to live a satisfying and meaningful life by practicing gratitude, engaging with others, setting new

objectives, and accepting progress.

CHAPTER 12:
Nothing is either good or bad

The idea that "nothing is either good or bad" stems from relativism and the recognition that evaluating events, acts, or circumstances is frequently subjective and context-dependent.
1. Perspective Relativity: - What one person considers "good" may not be the same for another due to personal experiences, beliefs, and values.
- Cultural, societal, and personal settings influence our perceptions of what is positive or unpleasant.
2. Complexity of Moral Values: - Moral and ethical issues differ between cultures and individuals.

- Actions identified as morally desirable in one setting may be seen differently in another, highlighting the subjective nature of moral judgments.
3. Unintended repercussions: - Positive activities can have negative repercussions, and vice versa.
- The complexities of outcomes highlight the difficulty of classifying situations as intrinsically good or negative.
4. possibilities for Personal Growth and Learning: - Despite being seen negatively, challenges and setbacks can provide possibilities for personal development.
- Adversity can build resilience, strength, and teach essential life lessons.
5. Changing Perspectives Over Time: - What was once negative might become a source of growth or good transformation in

the long run. - The fluidity of viewpoints emphasizes the changing aspect of evaluating occurrences.

6. Cognitive Biases: - Cognitive biases affect how people perceive and evaluate events.

- Recognizing and recognizing these biases is critical for appreciating the subjectivity inherent in classifying circumstances as good or poor.

7. Acceptance and Mindfulness: - Acceptance and mindfulness require noticing events without judgment. This technique allows people to enjoy the present moment without attaching a predetermined value to it.

8. Coping Mechanisms: - Viewing obstacles as opportunities can help nurture a positive mindset and navigate challenging situations. - This perspective shift highlights

the transformational power
of one's mentality.
The idea that "nothing is
either good or bad" is
consistent with many
philosophical and
psychological viewpoints,
prompting people to
examine their ingrained
beliefs in moral absolutism
and binary categorization.
Here are some extra factors
to consider:
1. Value in Neutrality: -
Accepting that events or
circumstances are neutral
unless assigned value
enables objective
assessment. - This
neutrality can serve as a
basis for clearer thinking
and decision-making.
2. Shades of Gray: - Life's
complexities typically exist
in shades of gray, rather
than clear black-and-white
differences.
- Recognizing the nuances
enables a more nuanced
and empathic

understanding of various situations.

3. Subjectivity of Experience: - Personal experiences impact perceptions, affecting how events are classified.
- Recognizing the subjective nature of these experiences encourages empathy and understanding for other viewpoints.

4. Philosophical Perspectives: - Taoism and Stoicism emphasize embracing life's uncertainties and avoiding inflexible judgments. - These ideas argue for a more balanced and equanimous response to both positive and negative occurrences.

5. Epistemic Humility: - Recognizing one's knowledge and understanding limits encourages epistemic humility. - This humility encourages people to approach circumstances

with an open mind and to consider other interpretations and views.
6. Coping with Ambiguity: - Life is unclear, and trying to categorize experiences can be frustrating.
- Developing a tolerance for ambiguity allows people to negotiate uncertainty more easily.
7. Cultural and ethical relativism emphasizes the diversity of values between societies and individuals.
- Recognizing these distinctions promotes a more inclusive and understanding approach to evaluating the moral landscape.
8. Narrative Reframing: - Cognitive reframing includes actively altering how events are mentally framed.
- This strategy can help people see problems as chances for growth.
9. Existential Perspective: - Existentialist thinkers, such

as Jean-Paul Sartre, believe in personal responsibility and the ability to decide the meaning of life.
- From this perspective, people are free to give their own values to experiences.
10. Balancing Positive and Negative: **- While accepting that nothing is intrinsically good or terrible, it is critical to appreciate the worth of happy experiences and the importance of dealing with truly damaging situations.
In essence, investigating the idea that "nothing is either good or bad" fosters a more nuanced, open-minded, and adaptable attitude to interpreting life's occurrences. Accepting the diversity and subjectivity of experiences can lead to a more nuanced understanding of the human condition and a more resilient mindset in the face of life's challenges.

CHAPTER 13:
How do you know what to do without thinking?

Knowing what to do without thinking usually means relying on instinct, intuition, or deeply ingrained behaviors. While these spontaneous responses can be useful in some instances, they may not always result in the most informed or ideal decisions. Here are some factors to consider:

1. **Instinctive Responses:** - Instincts are automatic reactions developed by humans and animals throughout existence.
- In acute or life-threatening situations, spontaneous reflexes can be critical to survival.
2. **Intuition:** - Intuition is a gut feeling or inner

understanding that does not require conscious reasoning. While intuition can help in decision-making, it is influenced by previous experiences and may not always result in objectively correct choices.

3. **Habitual Behavior:** - Habits are recurring activities that become automatic with time.
- Routine activities without conscious thought can be effective for jobs that do not demand extensive thought.

4. **Emotional Responses:** - Emotions can influence actions without conscious thought.
- Quick emotional responses can be useful in interpersonal circumstances, but they may not always coincide with rational decision-making.

5. **Implicit Learning:** - Individuals develop implicit knowledge and abilities via repeated exposure and

practice. This implicit learning adds to automatic responses in specific situations.
6. **Situational Awareness:** - Increased situational awareness enables quick responses to environmental cues without requiring extensive cognitive processing. This can be especially useful in dynamic or uncertain situations.
7. **Cultural and Social Influences:** - Cultural standards and social conditioning affect automatic responses to stimuli.
- People may act in accordance with society standards without consciously considering their choices.
8. **Pre-established Plans:** Having predetermined plans or routines for specific scenarios allows individuals

to behave without much thought.

- This method can be effective in well-practiced situations.

While automated responses offer advantages, they cannot be relied on entirely. They may not be appropriate for complicated problem solving, strategic decision-making, or circumstances requiring thorough consideration. Achieving a balance between instinctual impulses and deliberate thought is critical for making well-rounded and informed decisions in a range of situations.

CHAPTER 14:
How to follow your intuition

Tuning into your inner sensations and instincts to aid decision-making is an example of intuition. Here are some steps to help you connect with and follow your intuition:

1. Develop Self-Awareness:
- Regularly reflect on your ideas and emotions. Mindfulness techniques, such as meditation, can help you gain self-awareness and notice intuition cues.

2. Trust Your Gut Feeling: Intuition is typically expressed as a gut feeling or inner knowing.
- Learn to believe and acknowledge your feelings, even if they do not instantly correspond to logical thinking.

3. Quiet the Mind: - Incorporate quietness into your daily routine to reduce mental chatter.
- Silence helps your intuition to shine through without being distracted by extraneous forces.

4. Pay attention to physical sensations: - Observe how your body responds in

various situations. Physical sensations, such as tightness or relaxation, can indicate that your intuition is telling you something essential.

5. Reflect on Past Experiences:

- Recall times when trusting your intuition resulted in positive outcomes.

- Understanding how your intuition has previously benefited you might boost your confidence in its ability to guide you.

6. Distinguish Fear from Intuition: - Identify the difference between fear-based emotions and true intuitive advice.

- Fear is often caused by uncertainty, whereas intuition is a more subtle and persistent sensation of knowing.

7. Be Open to Possibilities: - Maintain an open mindset to gain intuitive insights.

- Avoid prior beliefs or biases that may impair your intuitive judgment.
8. Schedule quiet reflection time to connect with your inner ideas and emotions.
- Journaling can be an effective way to capture and analyze intuitive impressions.
9. Trust the Timing: - Intuitive direction may not always match your planned schedule.
- Be patient and believe that the correct decisions will come in their own time.
10. Practice Decision-Making: - Begin with modest decisions to develop your intuition.
- As your confidence in this approach grows, you'll be able to apply it to more important life decisions.
11. Listen to Your Emotions:
- Emotions can provide significant intuitive knowledge.
- Pay attention to feelings of excitement, discomfort, or

tranquility, as these can lead you to or away from specific decisions.

12. Be Open to Learning: - Maintain a mindset of constant learning and progress.

- Your intuition develops as you obtain new experiences and insights, so be open to honing your intuitive abilities.

By adopting these activities into your everyday routine, you can improve your capacity to trust your intuition. Balancing intuitive insights with rational reasoning enables a more comprehensive approach to decision-making, taking into account both inner wisdom and external factors.

CHAPTER 15:
Creating space for miracles

Creating space for miracles entails maintaining an open

and receptive mindset, promoting positive energy, and allowing for unexpected, transformative events to occur. Here are the steps to bring miracles into your life:

1. Believe in Possibility: - Develop a mindset that believes amazing things can happen.

- Develop a belief in the possibility of positive and unexpected events.

2. Release Limiting Beliefs:

- Recognize and let go of any limiting beliefs that may prevent you from experiencing miracles.

- Confront negative beliefs that undermine your faith in good progress.

3. Practice Gratitude: - Develop a grateful mindset by recognizing and appreciating positive parts in your life.

- Gratitude generates positive energy, which invites other positive experiences.

4. Visualize Success: -
Create mental images of
desired outcomes.
- Visualization improves
your focus and directs your
energy toward positive
possibilities.
5. Set Positive Intentions: -
Define your goals and
aspirations with positive
intent.
- Express your intentions
clearly and enthusiastically,
confirming your commitment
to positive change.
6. Embrace Uncertainty: -
Allow for the unknown and
unexpected.
- Miracles frequently occur
in circumstances of
uncertainty, so be prepared
for the unpredictable aspect
of life.
7. Be open to surprises.
- Stay open to unexpected
chances and surprises.
- Approach life with curiosity
and a desire to discover
new possibilities.

8. To connect with the present moment, practice mindfulness.
- Presence enables you to recognize subtle possibilities and serendipitous situations.
9. Let Go of Control: - Eliminate the urge for rigorous control over all aspects of your life.
- Believe that the cosmos has a unique way of organizing positive outcomes.
10. Practice Patience: - Miracles may not come right away; they typically take their own time.
- Be patient and trust the process, even if things appear unsure.
11. Surround yourself with positivity by creating an environment that promotes it.
- Surround yourself with people, experiences, and influences that encourage and inspire you.

12. Recognize and cherish minor marvels in everyday life.
- Appreciating the minor wonders prepares the way for larger, unexpected miracles.
13. Demonstrate faith and trust: - Believe in the possibilities of positive transformation.
- Believe in your power to overcome obstacles and embrace miraculous transformations.
14. Act with Kindness: - Show kindness and charity to others.
- Positive actions frequently spread throughout the interwoven web of life, making room for miracles to occur.
By incorporating these techniques into your thought and lifestyle, you create the conditions for miracles to occur. Miracles frequently occur when you link your ideas, actions, and energies

with the possibility of great and extraordinary events.

CHAPTER 16:
What happens when you begin living in non-thinking (potential obstacles) ?

Living in a state of non-thinking, while seductive, can create significant problems and challenges that may have an impact on many facets of your life. Here are some considerations.
1. Impulsive Decision-Making: - Lack of thought might result in impulsive decisions influenced by emotions or desires, rather than deliberate consideration.
- Impulsivity might have negative consequences and jeopardize long-term ambitions.

2. Lack of Strategic
Planning: - Effective
strategic planning involves
careful consideration and
analysis.
- Living in a non-thinking
state may result in a lack of
foresight and planning,
making it difficult to manage
complex situations.
3. Difficulty in Problem-
Solving: - Problem-solving
often requires cognitive
involvement and critical
thinking.
- A non-thinking approach
may hinder your ability to
successfully solve problems
and devise innovative
solutions.
4. Strained Relationships:
Effective communication
and understanding in
relationships require
thorough consideration of
others' opinions.
- Non-thinking conduct can
result in misunderstandings,
disputes, and strained
relationships with those
around you.

5. Risk of overlooking consequences:
- Failure to think can lead to an inability to consider the possible outcomes of actions.
- Failure to anticipate outcomes may have unintended negative consequences, affecting both personal and professional parts of life.
6. Personal progress Stagnation: - Self-reflection, learning, and intentional development are key to achieving continuous progress.
- Living without thoughtful consideration may limit your ability to progress and reach your greatest potential.
7. Missed Opportunities: - Opportunities for learning, growth, and advancement may be ignored without intentional thought.
- Non-thinking behavior may result in missed opportunities for personal

and professional
development.
8. Ineffective
Communication: - Effective
communication involves
considering the audience,
context, and message.
- Non-thinking
communication can lack
clarity, resulting in
misunderstandings and
misinterpretations.
9. Reduced Adaptability: -
Adaptability is essential for
navigating change and
uncertainty.
- Non-Thinking conduct may
result in resistance to
change, making it difficult to
adapt to changing
circumstances.
10. Reduced
Emotional **Regulation:** -
Emotional regulation is the
process of understanding
and managing one's
emotions.
- Non-thinking can lead to
impulsive emotional
reactions that harm

personal well-being and relationships.

11. Challenges in accomplishing **objectives**: -
Setting and accomplishing objectives requires strategic preparation and thought.

- Non-thinking may impede your capacity to plan practical measures toward your goals.

In essence, while non-thinking might provide a reprieve from overthinking, it is critical to achieve a balance. Incorporating careful analysis into decision-making, planning, and communication enables a more comprehensive and flexible approach to life's difficulties. Balancing spontaneity and mindfulness helps you overcome challenges and produces excellent outcomes in the long run.

Conclusion:

Finally, "Don't Accept Every Thought That Comes to Your Mind" encourages readers on a transforming journey of self-awareness, questioning their automatic acceptance of thoughts and beliefs. The book promotes mindfulness, urging people to question and explore their cognitive processes. Readers may negotiate life with better clarity and openness if they understand the power of perspective and the influence of cognitive biases. Finally, the book serves as a reminder that our thoughts are not absolute truths, and that taking a more attentive attitude can lead to a better understanding of oneself and a more full and meaningful existence.